AUSTRALIAN DENTAL ASSOCIATION

Tooth-friendly treats

20 recipes recommended by dentists

Profits from the Australian Dental Association's sales of the Tooth-friendly Treats recipe book are donated to the Australian Dental Health Foundation (ADHF).

The ADHF works with charities and not-for-profit organisations around Australia to provide access to essential dental care for disadvantaged members of the community. The Foundation coordinates the delivery of pro bono dental treatment through volunteer programs such as the Rebuilding Smiles® program which helps people who've experienced domestic violence and who may have immediate dental trauma or ongoing oral health problems from a lack of dental treatment over time.

The Foundation also provides community service grants in combination with the Mars Wrigley Foundation, and together with the Dental Hygienists' Association of Australia, it offers Indigenous Study Grants for Indigenous students undertaking studies to become a dental hygienist or oral health therapist.

For more information about ADHF, go to: *https://www.adhf.org.au*

ISBN: 978-0-646-82347-8

Copyright © 2020 Australian Dental Association, All rights reserved.

AUSTRALIAN DENTAL ASSOCIATION

Tooth-friendly treats

20 recipes recommended by dentists

········ Foreword ········

Treats. Yum! Doesn't everyone like a sweet treat every now and then? I certainly do.

I am a chef. I enjoy food and love restaurants. My wife is a Dental Hygienist so I also have an interest in good dental health.

I began cooking in professional kitchens over 30 years ago now. My training as a chef then was to cook food that was tasty and looked good. We would compete among our own brigade and with all the other top restaurants to make the tastiest and most attractive dishes around. Fat is flavour and sugar is too.

Now in 2020, restaurants still compete to have the best dish but society is more aware of what we are putting into our bodies. At home, I too am conscious of what my family and I are eating. Don't get me wrong - I still love fats, sugars and tasty food! But now I acknowledge that it's an occasional treat. When I do eat it, I make sure I enjoy it. Generally I try and eat mostly unpackaged foods and limit sugar, especially in drinks.

Australian's diet has changed over the past 30 years. Foods have become more processed and readily available. Obesity is increasing and so is tooth decay.

This cookbook has 20 low sugar recipes for tooth-friendly treats, collected from dental professionals all over the country. There are also some tips including recommended added sugar daily intake (24g – that's only 6 teaspoons!), hidden sugars and navigating through misleading labels. A bowl of "healthy" cereal can contain 25% sugar - crazy!

You will notice in these recipes that often if you use fruit, or dried fruit there is no need for added sugar. These contain natural sugars which you also need to be mindful of but don't count in your 24 grams a day. I love the pancakes with strawberries or bananas. The pikelets are a winner too.

I think it's great that people are thinking about food more now. What's in it, where it comes from, how to cook and present it and also what it's doing to our bodies and teeth.

Have a look through at these tooth-friendly recipes and tips - and enjoy!

Scott Pickett
Director and Chef
Pickett & Co.
pickettandco.com

Contents

Judges	8
A Word About Portion Control	9
Homemade Toasted Muesli	10
Fruity Pikelets	11
Soybean Pudding	12
Banana on Banana on Banana Pancakes	13
Date Rolls	14
Rujak with Tamarillo	15
Get Sugar Savvy	Hidden Sugars	16
Sesame Biscuit	17
Go-to Birthday Cake	18
Get Sugar Savvy	Sugar Maths	19
Coco Caramelised Collection	20
Get Sugar Savvy	Sugary Drinks	22
French Earl Grey Panna Cotta	23
Easy No-Bake Cinnamon Doughnuts	24
Get Sugar Savvy	Understanding Sugar	25
Strawberry Galette	26
Apricot and Oat Balls	27
Chocolate Rice Cakes	28
Banana Delight	29
Delicious Ice Cream	30
Berry Pancakes	31
Homemade Spiced Granola	32
Get Sugar Savvy	Read The Label	33
Vegan Banana Bread	34
Chia-ful Cups	35
Get Sugar Savvy	Sugar and its Effects on Teeth	36
Acknowledgment	37

.... Judges ....

Jemma O'Hanlon
Accredited Practising Dietitian

As a dietitian, Jemma has always been a lover of good food. Jemma was in the kitchen from a young age, experimenting with new recipes and finding ways to make them healthier. Now a Director of Dietitians Australia and R&D Manager at not-for-profit research and development corporation Hort Innovation, Jemma oversees the nutrition research which supports Aussie growers. Jemma recently appeared on Channel 10's **My Market Kitchen**, showing Australians how easy it can be to whip up delicious meals from local produce. Connect with Jemma on Instagram at @jemmaohanlon.

Dr Matt Hopcraft
CEO of the Australian Dental Association Victorian Branch

Matt Hopcraft is a dental public health expert and CEO of the Australian Dental Association Victorian Branch. He co-founded SugarFree Smiles to advocate for measures to improve oral health in Australia and has been involved with many public campaigns to raise awareness of oral health issues and encourage healthy eating. Matt appeared as a contestant on **MasterChef Australia** in 2015, placing sixth.

Image courtesy of Kylie Mibus

Eithne Irving
Deputy Chief Executive Officer and General Manager of Policy at the Australian Dental Association

Eithne is the Deputy Chief Executive Officer and General Manager of Policy at the Australian Dental Association and a registered nurse. Her role involves managing a broad portfolio including advocacy, oral health promotion and public relations. A previous member of the Dietetics Credentialing Council for eight years and current chair of the NSW Board of the National Nursing and Midwifery Board of Australia, she understands only too well the impact sugar is having on teeth and the general health of the community. Eithne can be credited with the idea for developing the cookbook and is delighted to see it come to fruition.

Dr Mikaela Chinotti
Oral Health Promoter at the Australian Dental Association

Dr Mikaela Chinotti is a practising general dentist. She is the Oral Health Promoter at the Australian Dental Association, where one of her main roles is overseeing the planning and implementation of the Dental Health Week campaign. Mikaela took the concept of the cookbook from an idea to a reality. Connect with Mikaela on Instagram at @dentist_mikaela.

A Word About
Portion Control

We hope you enjoy these tooth-friendly recipes with your family and friends. Keep in mind that portion control is always key when it comes to enjoying sweet foods. The World Health Organisation recommends limiting added sugars to 5% of the total energy intake. Discretionary foods, in line with the Australian Dietary Guidelines, are not essential as part of a healthy balanced diet, but may be enjoyed occasionally and in small portions.

A discretionary serve, for example, is 2 scoops of ice cream (75g), 1 slice of cake (40g) or a couple of sweet biscuits. Be sure to practise mindful eating and savour every mouthful when enjoying these sweet treats.

Your dentist can discuss with you about the types of foods that are more likely to contribute to tooth decay and you may also wish to discuss your diet with a dietitian. Accredited Practising Dietitians are the university-qualified experts in nutrition who can tailor advice based on your individual needs.

To find an Accredited Practising Dietitian, visit **dietitiansaustralia.org.au**
To find a dentist, visit **ada.org.au/findadentist**

Castle Cove Family Dental's

········ Homemade Toasted Muesli ········

Place the toasted muesli in brown bags or jars to make a great gift.

 10 mins preparation
15 mins baking

 Makes 37.5 serves
Serving size: 40g

 Sugar per serve: 3.6g
Sugar per 100g: 9.11g

Ingredients

1kg rolled oats
250g pepitas/pumpkin seeds
250g slithered almonds
100g sesame seeds

6 pitted dates, finely sliced
3 tablespoons honey
½ cup olive oil
½ cup shredded coconut

1. Pre-heat the oven to 180°C (fan-forced).

2. Combine all dry ingredients in a large bowl.

3. Add the olive oil and honey and combine.

4. Spread mixture over large flat baking trays.

5. Bake in oven for 15 minutes or until lightly toasted.

6. Allow to cool and place in an airtight container.

Castle Cove Family Dental's

Fruity Pikelets

A tooth-friendly, low-sugar recipe, great for brunch or after-school snacks.

 15 mins   Makes 14 pikelets / Serving size: 2 pikelets   Sugar per serve: 2g / Sugar per 100g: 3.4g

Ingredients

Pikelet mix
2 cups self-raising flour
2 cups milk
2 eggs
Pinch sugar
Pinch salt

Cream
400ml cream
1 teaspoon vanilla bean paste

Garnish
Fresh fruit such as strawberries, banana, kiwifruit and blueberries

1. Mix the pikelet ingredients until combined.
2. Pour spoonfuls of batter onto a lightly greased frypan at a medium heat.
3. Cook for 30 seconds per side or until cooked through. Keep warm.
4. Whip cream to stiff peaks then add vanilla bean paste.
5. Top the pikelets with the whipped cream and fresh fruit garnish.

Castle Cove Family Dental

Dr Mary Moss and the team at Castle Cove Family Dental are a family-friendly and community-orientated dental practice located in Castle Cove, NSW.

Dr Amanda Phoon Nguyen's
Soybean Pudding - (Tofu Pudding, Dou Hua)

A silky-smooth soy pudding that is a popular Chinese treat.

 15 mins preparation
Overnight to set

 Serves 4
Serving size: 80g

 Dairy-free

 Gluten-free

 Sugar per serve: 1.9g
Sugar per 100g: 2.5g

Ingredients

3 cups unsweetened soy milk (720ml)
Note: you can either make your own by blending rehydrated soy beans with water, or buy this from the store. If using the store-bought version, it is the important that the only ingredients are soybeans, and water.
2 teaspoons gelatin
(Optional) 3 tablespoons ginger, crushed

Dr Amanda Phoon Nguyen

Dr Amanda Phoon Nguyen is an Oral Medicine Specialist at Perth Oral Medicine and Dental Sleep Centre in Western Australia. Follow Dr Nguyen on Instagram at @oralmedicineoralpathology for oral medicine tidbits.

Toppings
Cut fruit
1 cup unsweetened soy milk

> **Topping variations:**
> *Sugar-free syrup (1:1 mix xylitol and water): Bring the mixture to a boil and allow to simmer until the xylitol has dissolved into the water, creating a syrup. Pandan leaves may be included in the mixture as it boils. Remove the leaves before serving.*

1. Prepare 4 small containers for the pudding to set in.

2. Pour unsweetened soy milk in a medium-sized saucepan. Sprinkle gelatin over and allow to bloom undisturbed for a few minutes.

3. Heat over gentle heat for 5 minutes, stirring continuously. Do not allow to boil. Add the crushed ginger if you desire. Remove from heat.

4. Strain mixture using a sieve into the 4 containers and allow bubbles to settle.

5. Place in the refrigerator for at least 8 hours or overnight to set.

6. Serve with your choice of toppings. Enjoy chilled, or warmed!

Margaret Tran's
Banana on Banana on Banana Pancakes

Get creative in your pancake toppings. Tooth-friendly options can include chia seeds, peanut butter, sliced fresh fruit, almonds and shredded coconut.

 20 mins   Makes 8 pancakes
Serving size: 100g

 Sugar per serve: 7.6g
Sugar per 100g: 7.6g

Ingredients

Banana Yoghurt
1 banana
2 tablespoons plain Greek yoghurt
1 tablespoon milk

Notes: The riper the bananas, the sweeter your pancakes.

Pancakes
1 banana
1 egg
⅓ cup self-raising flour (white or wholemeal)
1 cup quick oats
½ cup milk
1 tablespoon cinnamon

Caramelised Banana
1 banana
Cinnamon

1. For the 'yoghurt', blend the banana, yoghurt and milk together. Pour into a bowl and set aside.

2. For the pancakes, blend the banana, egg, flour, oats, milk and cinnamon together.

3. Spray a light coat of oil onto a non-stick pan and place on a medium heat.

4. Spoon 2 tablespoons of the pancake mixture and flatten into a circular pancake shape. Cook each side on medium heat for approximately 2 minutes until it looks lightly golden-brown. A lid can be used to cover the pan to cook the pancakes faster.

5. Once the pancakes are cooked, use the same pan to caramelise the bananas. Slice the banana, place pieces flat in the pan and sprinkle with cinnamon. When juices begin sizzling out and the cooked side is golden-brown, flip the pieces. This should take about 1-2 minutes on each side.

6. Jazz up your pancakes with the yoghurt and caramelised banana.

Margaret Tran

Margaret Tran is a 4th-year dental student at La Trobe Dental School, Bendigo in Victoria. Follow Margaret on Instagram at @dental_foodie.

Dr Karuna Khatri's
Date Rolls

Enjoy these date rolls as a snack, a healthy dessert or paired with cheese.

 20 mins preparation
Overnight to set

 Makes 3-4 rolls
Serving size: 2 pieces (40g)

 Gluten-free

 Sugar per serve: 10.2g
Sugar per 100g: 25.5g

Ingredients

200g pitted fresh dates
1 tablespoon ghee/clarified butter/butter
2 tablespoons finely chopped almonds
2 tablespoons finely chopped pistachios
2 tablespoons finely chopped cashews
1-2 tablespoons desiccated coconut

(Optional) 2-3 dried finely chopped figs can be added, however this increases the sugar content of the recipe.

1. Finely dice the pitted fresh dates.

2. Melt the ghee or butter, add the dates and cook on the stove over a low heat for approximately 3 minutes.

3. Place the cooked dates into a medium-sized bowl. Add the chopped almonds, pistachios and cashews. The mixture should gather into a soft ball.

4. Roll the mixture into log rolls 2cm in diameter.

5. Roll the log rolls in the desiccated coconut.

6. Refrigerate the log rolls until set firm and cool.

7. When cool, use a sharp knife to cut the rolls into 5mm-thick discs.

Dr Karuna Khatri

Dr Karuna Khatri is the Principal Dentist and owner of Dental Pearls by Karuna Khatri in Brisbane Queensland. She and her team have been caring for the oral health of their local community for 16 years.

Dr Epita Pane's
Rujak with Tamarillo

A spicy fruit salad with tamarillo dressing.

 20 mins   Serving size fruit: 150g
Serving size dressing: 15ml

 Vegan   Gluten-free

 Dressing:
Sugar per serve: 2.4g
Sugar per 100g: 16.1g

Ingredients

Dressing
2 pieces green bird's eye chilli
1/3 young green plantain with skin
100g palm sugar
4 tamarillos (skin removed)
½ teaspoon of salt

Fruits
100g pineapple
100g sweet potato
100g young green papaya
100g brown nashi pear
100g jicama

For garnish (optional)
3 tablespoons fried peanuts, roughly chopped

1. Slice the fruits into bite-sized pieces.

2. To make the dressing, use a mortar and pestle or a food processor to crush/combine the bird's eye chilli and salt.

3. Combine the palm sugar (roughly chopped) and chopped young plantain with the chill and salt mixture. Note: for a runnier dressing, dissolve the palm sugar in boiling water. Cover the sugar with enough water until it dissolves.

4. Finally, add the tamarillo to the dressing mixture and blend to combine.

5. (Optional) Add the chopped peanuts to the sauce.

Dr Epita Pane

Dr Pane is an endodontist working in the Royal Dental Hospital of Melbourne. She is a mother of 4 boys who love to cook together, trying new recipes and recreating childhood favourites.

Get Sugar Savvy
Hidden Sugars

We usually think of sugar as the white granules we spoon into coffee and tea or add to baking recipes. But sugar comes in many forms and they can all contribute to tooth decay.

Sugar can be called more than 50 different names, making it hard to detect on food and drink labels. These are known as **hidden sugars**.

Common names for sugar

Agave nectar	Brown sugar	Cane juice	Cane sugar	Caster sugar
Coconut sugar	Caramel	Corn syrup	Date sugar	Dextrose
Fructose	Fruit juice	Fruit juice concentrate	Glucose	Golden syrup
High fructose corn syrup	Honey	Icing sugar	Malt syrup	Maltodextrin
Maltose	Maple syrup	Molasses	Palm sugar	Raw sugar
Rice Malt	Saccharose	Sucrose	Syrup	Treacle

Look out for these names on the ingredient list of nutrition information panels when shopping. Even foods and drinks which claim to have no added or refined sugars, can contain a lot of sugar. The closer the ingredient is to the top of the ingredient list, the more of it is present in the food or drink.

Gordon Dental Practice's
Sesame Biscuit - A savoury and sweet treat

A biscuit recipe with sugar-free ingredients that can be enjoyed by all ages, from toddlers up to seniors.

 15 mins preparation
25 mins baking
15 mins cooling

 Makes 8 biscuits
Serving size: 2 biscuits (40g)

 Dairy-free

 Sugar per serve: less than 1g
Sugar per 100g: less than 1g

Ingredients

30g semolina
60g sesame seeds
30g plain flour
40g xylitol

1 egg
30g olive oil
15g slivered almonds
10g chia seeds
3 drops of vanilla essence

1. Pre-heat the oven to 150°C (fan-forced).

2. Place all the ingredients in a bowl and mix with a hand mixer.

3. Line an oven tray with greaseproof baking paper.

4. Brush a thin layer of olive oil on the baking paper, just enough to line the tray. Dab the extra olive oil with a paper towel.

5. Pour the mixture on to the baking tray and spread it gently with a spatula to make it an even layer approximately 3mm in thickness.

6. Bake in the oven for 25 minutes.

7. Once baked, let the mixture cool for about 15 minutes then cut into squares.

Dr Marion D'Souza, Dr Joyce Lau and team at Gordon Dental Practice

Dr Marion D'Souza, Dr Joyce Lau and the team at Gordon Dental Practice, Gordon NSW, have a focus on family dental care and preventative services.

Sesame Biscuit

The Dental Gallery's
Go-to Birthday Cake

Just what the dentist called for, a tooth-friendly chocolate cake! This cake has been used for 16 years as The Dental Gallery's birthday celebration cake.

 15 mins preparation
45 mins baking
30 mins cooling

 Serves 8 slices
Serving size: 1 slice (80g)

 Gluten-free

 Dairy-free

 Sugar per serve: 1.8g
Sugar per 100g: 2.3g

Ingredients

3 cups almond meal
½ cup cocoa powder
2 tablespoons gluten-free cornflour
2 teaspoons gluten-free baking powder
1 cup unsweetened almond milk
½ cup monkfruit sweetener
¼ cup grapeseed oil
1 tablespoon vanilla extract
2 eggs

1. Pre-heat the oven to 175°C (fan-forced).
2. Grease and line a 20cm round cake tin.
3. Combine almond meal, cocoa powder, cornflour and baking powder.
4. Add the milk, monkfruit sweetener, oil, vanilla and eggs, mix until combined.
5. Pour the mixture into the cake tin and bake for 45 minutes.
6. Cool in the tin for 30 minutes, then turn out and allow cake to continue to cool.

Icing

1 avocado
2 teaspoons vanilla extract
¼ cup cocoa powder
¼ cup monkfruit sweetner

1. Combine all the ingredients for the icing. Mix until smooth and no avocado lumps remain.
2. Spread evenly over the top and sides of the cake.

The Dental Gallery

This recipe is a creation of the team at The Dental Gallery, located in Point Cook, Victoria, who have been providing quality dental care and customer service in Point Cook since 2004.

Go-to Birthday Cake

Get Sugar Savvy
Sugar maths

1 teaspoon = 4 grams

Recommended daily sugar limit = 6 teaspoons or 24 grams

Hidden sugars in everyday foods can cause your sugar consumption to add up quickly...

Fruit juice **Breakfast cereal** **Sugar in coffee** **Muesli bars**

Did you know a glass of juice and bowl of cereal for breakfast can equal 6 or more teaspoons of sugar?

Nutrition Information		
Serves per packing: 30		
Serve size: 20ml		
	Quantity per serving	Quantity per 100ml
Energy	180kJ	900kJ
Protein	0.4g	2g
Fat, total	0.01g	0.06g
- Saturated	0.004g	0.2g
Carbohydrates	12g	60g
- Sugars	10g	55g
Sodium	200mg	1000mg
Ingredients	Sugar, Tomato Puree, Water, Thickener, Salt, Food Acids, Maltodextrin, Molasses, Natural Flavours, Spices, Vegetable Gum	
All quantities above are average		

How to find added sugar:

Most labels do not point out the added sugars. To identify any added sugars present, look at the list of ingredients.

In this example, sugar, maltodextrin and molasses are names that represent sugar. The nearer the ingredient is to the top of the list, the more present in the food or drink. In this item, sugar is the number one ingredient.

How to know if you should look for a healthier alternative?

Look at the value for sugar per 100 grams. If the number is greater than 15 grams, consider finding an alternative with a lower sugar content.

Ideally look for foods and drinks with less than 5 grams per 100 grams of sugar, but less than 10 grams is acceptable.

How to calculate the number of teaspoons of sugar:

Divide the grams of sugar by 4. Each teaspoon of sugar equals 4 grams.

Example. There are 10 grams of sugar present per serve.

$$\frac{\text{10 grams per serve}}{\text{4 grams per teaspoon}} = \text{2.5 teaspoons of sugar}$$

Caroline Mastry and Ernesto Villalba's
········ Coco Caramelised Collection ········

This delicious tooth-friendly dessert option is too fancy to not impress.

 35 mins

 Makes 6 serves
Serving size: 200g

 Gluten-free

 Sugar per serve: 11.5g
Sugar per 100g: 5.7g

Ingredients

Caramel Sauce
¼ cup pitted dates
Pinch of salt
¼ cup water

1. Soak the dates in water and a pinch of salt for approximately 10 minutes (the longer the better).
2. Blend the dates and water until smooth.
3. Set aside ready for assembly.

Cookie Crumble Base
¼ cup pecans
2 teaspoons cinnamon
1 teaspoon nutmeg
½ teaspoon cloves
4 teaspoons cocoa
30g butter
1 tablespoon banana flour
2 tablespoons artificial sweetener

Use an artifical sweetener such as monkfruit sweetener or xylitol.

1. Crush pecans in a small bowl.
2. Add spices (cinnamon, nutmeg and cloves) to the pecans and mix well.
3. Stir in artificial sweetener, banana flour and cocoa.
4. Rub in butter with the dry ingredients.
5. Place on a baking tray and toast for 5-10 minutes (or until rich brown colour).
6. Set aside ready for assembly.

Mousse
6 eggs
2 cups coconut milk
2 teaspoons artificial sweetener
3 ripe bananas

1. Separate the eggs.
2. Beat the egg yolks with the coconut milk.
3. Add the mashed banana and sugar substitute to the bowl.
4. Transfer the mixture to a saucepan and warm over a low to medium heat.
5. Whisk in 2 teaspoons of artificial sweetener.
6. While the custard is warming, in a separate bowl beat egg whites until they form soft peaks and set aside.
7. Remove custard mix from heat.
8. Using a spatula gently fold the egg whites into the custard mixture.

To assemble

1. Using glass jars or cups, place 1 tablespoon of the cookie crumble bases evenly on the base of each.

2. Spoon the mousse over the cookie crumble base, spreading the mixture evenly between the 6 jars or cups.

3. Spoon 1 tablespoon of caramel sauce evenly over the mousse.

To garnish (optional)

1. Consider garnishing with slivered almonds, fresh raspberries, coconut cream or sliced banana.

Caroline Mastry and Ernesto Villalba

Caroline Mastry and Ernesto Villalba are dental students at the School of Dentistry and Oral Health, Griffith University on Queensland's Gold Coast.

Get Sugar Savvy
Sugary drinks

How do they stack up?

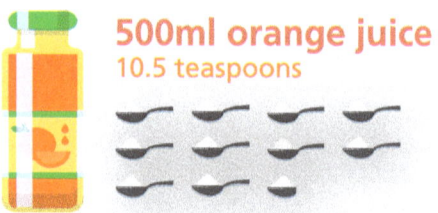
500ml orange juice
10.5 teaspoons

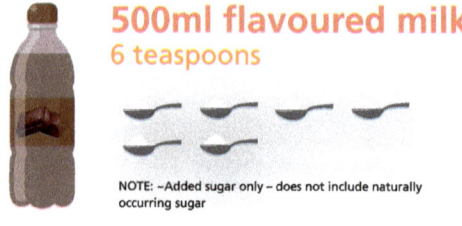
500ml flavoured milk
6 teaspoons
NOTE: ~Added sugar only – does not include naturally occurring sugar

600ml soft drink
16 teaspoons

375ml can = 10 teaspoons

600ml sports drink
8.5 teaspoons

500ml energy drinks
16 teaspoons

^Energy drink sugar teaspoon content is an average

Water
0 sugar!

Water and unflavoured milk drinks are the best

Recommended daily added sugar limit to decrease risk of tooth decay

6 teaspoons or 24 grams

Dr Elice Chen's
········ French Earl Grey Panna Cotta ········

A new take on an old favourite, this panna cotta recipe is vegan, dairy free and sure to delight.

 10 mins preparation
3 hours setting time

 Makes 4 serves
Serving size: 125g

 Dairy-free

 Vegan

 Nut-free

 Sugar per serve: 4.3g
Sugar per 100g: 3.5g

Ingredients

500ml soy milk
3-4 heaped teaspoons or teabags of Earl Grey tea (to taste)
½ teaspoom vanilla extract
¾ teaspoon powdered agar
4 teaspoons maple syrup

To make the panna cotta

1. Gently heat soy milk, tea, vanilla and agar in small saucepan until it boils, stirring with a wooden spoon or spatula to prevent sticking.

2. Remove the tea by straining or taking out the teabags.

3. Pour into ramekins or cups and put in fridge.
It should set in 3 hours but you can leave it overnight to be sure.

Dr Elice Chen

Dr Elice Chen is a general dentist passionate about preventive care, working at Brighter Smiles Family Dental Care, Ringwood and Mitcham in Victoria. Follow Dr Chen on Instagram at @the_naked_tooth.

To serve

1. Unmould the panna cotta by sliding a knife around the edge of the ramekin, pressing the panna cotta gently to break the seal. Flip it onto a plate.

2. Drizzle one teaspoon of maple syrup over the top of the panna cotta.

3. Optional: decorate with some edible lavender or rose petals. These can be plucked from fresh flowers or sometimes can be found in tea blends.

French Earl Grey Panna Cotta

Dr Valeriya Matveeva's

Easy No-Bake Cinnamon Doughnuts

This recipe can be eaten raw as a doughnut or throw them in the oven for 15-20 mins to get a batch of delicious soft cookies.

 10 mins

 Makes 14-15 doughnuts
Serving size: 2 doughnuts (30g)

 Gluten-free

 Dairy-free

 Vegan

 Sugar per serve: 1g
Sugar per 100g: 3.3g

Ingredients

150g almond meal
2 tablespoons melted coconut oil
1 tablespoon flaxmeal
2 tablespoons water
¼ cup monkfruit/erythritol sweetener (granules)
2 teaspoons ground cinnamon
Pinch of salt
½ teaspoon sugar-free vanilla essence

For coating
1 teaspoon ground cinnamon
2 teaspoons monkfruit sweetener

Dr Valeriya Matveeva

Dr Valeriya Mateeva is a practising general dentist in Sydney, NSW. Follow Dr Mateeva on Instagram at @dentalligence.

1. Combine almond meal, cinnamon, sweetener and salt, mix with a spoon and set aside.

2. In a smaller bowl, mix flaxmeal and water, and leave for a minute to thicken (this will be sticky to replace an egg).

3. Combine the melted coconut oil, vanilla essence and the wet flaxmeal and water mixture, mix together and place on top of the almond meal dry mix.

4. Mix ingredients together until smooth. Note: it will initially look like there is not enough 'wet' part to cover the 'dry' mix. It's okay! Fluffy almond meal mixes very nicely with the coconut oil under firm hand pressure.

5. Pinching a small amount of dough, roll it between your hands into nice round balls.

6. In a separate bowl or plate, mix the ground cinnamon and granulated sweetener. Roll each 'doughnuts' to coat evenly, and voilà - it's all ready to eat!

7. To turn the doughnuts into cookies, pre-heat the oven to 180°C. Place the doughnuts on an oven tray lined with baking paper and place in the oven for 15-20 minutes.

Get Sugar Savvy
Understanding sugar

Quantity of nutrient per serving
Serving sizes differ between products. This is not a good reference when comparing products.

Sugar per serve
In this product there are 3 serves and each contains 18.6grams (g) of sugar

Where does sugar sit in the list?
The closer to the top of the list of ingredients, the more sugar is present.

Nutrition Information		
Servings per package: 3 Serving size: 150g		
	Quantity per serving	Quantity per 100g
Energy	608kJ	405 kJ
Protein	4.2g	2.8g
Fat, total	7.4g	4.9g
- Saturated	4.5g	3.0g
Carbohydrate, total	18.6g	12.4g
- Sugars	18.6g	12.4g
Sodium	90mg	60mg
Ingredients:	Whole milk, concentrated skim milk, sugar, banana (8%), strawberry (6%), grape (4%), peach (2%), pineapple (2%), gelatine, culture, thickener (1442)	
All quantities above are averages		

Use this column when comparing products

How much sugar to look for:
- 15g or less → okay
- 10g or less → better
- 5g or less → best

Daily sugar consumption

Limit added sugar intake to 6 or less teaspoons per day. This equals 24 grams of added sugar or less.

- 1 teaspoon sugar = 4 grams sugar

Comparing products

Use the 'per 100g' column. This allows you to compare 'apples with apples.'

- Aim for less than 10 grams of sugar per 100 grams, but less than 5 grams is best. Foods claiming 'no added sugar' often contain a higher level of sugar from natural sources but these sugars can still cause tooth decay.

Don't forget
- Brush with a fluoride toothpaste.
- Clean between your teeth with floss or interdental brushes.
- See a dentist regularly to maintain good oral health.

North Adelaide Dental Care's
Strawberry Galette

Impress at brunch by serving these quick and easy, tooth-friendly fruit and pastry sweet treats.

 15 mins preparation
10-15 mins baking

 Makes 4 galettes
Serving size: 1 galette (90g)

 Sugar per serve: 3.3g
Sugar per 100g: 3.7g

Ingredients

1 semi-thawed puff pastry sheet
8 medium-sized strawberries, mashed
8 medium-sized strawberries, thinly sliced
A handful of fresh blueberries

1. Pre-heat the oven to 180°C (fan-forced).

2. Using a pastry cutter or small knife, cut the puff pastry sheet into quarters.

3. Fold over the edges of the pastry squares to create 1cm borders.

4. In a small saucepan, cook the mashed strawberries with a dash of water over a medium heat for approximately 2 minutes to create a strawberrry purée.

5. Place 1 teaspoon of strawberry purée into the centre of each puff pastry quarter and smooth the purée out to the border edges.

6. Place sliced strawberries over the centre of each pastry quarter, adding a few blueberries between strawberry slices.

7. Bake for 10-15 minutes or until lightly golden brown.

North Adelaide Dental Care's
.... Apricot and Oat Balls ....

Pack one of these nut-free, dairy-free balls for a mid-morning snack - they are sure to delight.

 15 mins   Makes 13 balls, Serving size: 1 ball (40g)   Dairy-free   Nut-free   Sugar per serve: 7.3g, Sugar per 100g: 18.3g

Ingredients

1 cup oats
1 cup dried apricots
½ cup pitted dates
¾ cup desiccated coconut

1 teaspoon vanilla essence
1 cup water (as needed)

1. Measure all dry ingredients into a mixing bowl.

2. Place into a food processor, add vanilla essence and blend well.

3. Gradually add water until mixture forms clumps.

4. Remove mixture from food processor. Roll the mixture into bite-sized balls.

5. Store in fridge or freezer to chill.

North Adelaide Dental Care

The North Adelaide Dental Care team, located in North Adelaide, has been serving the Adelaide and South Australia community for more than 30 years.

Dr Sitanshu Arora's
········ Chocolate Rice Cakes ········

A great morning or afternoon tea snack that is both sweet and savoury.

 15 mins   Vegan   Gluten-free   Makes 3 rice cakes
Serving size: 1 rice cake (40g)   Sugar per serve: 8.3g
Sugar per 100g: 20.7g

Ingredients

30g '70% cocoa' dark chocolate
15g pumpkin seeds
15g sunflower seeds
15g goji berries
15 gms dry roasted almonds
10gms hemps seeds
3 brown rice cakes

Dr Sitanshu Arora

Dr Sitanshu Arora is a general dentist who is based in Melbourne, Victoria. She is a mother of one who enjoys cooking low-sugar treats for the family.

1. Melt dark chocolate in a bowl over hot water.

2. Spread the melted chocolate on the rice cakes then sprinkle with toppings.

3. Place the rice cakes in the fridge for 10 minutes for the chocolate to set.

Remarkable Dentistry's
Banana Delight

This dish is nut free, egg free and lactose free, great for teeth but also great for people with allergies.

 15 mins

 Makes 8 pieces
Serving size: 80g

 Lactose-free

 Nut-free

 Sugar per serve: 6.8g
Sugar per 100g: 8.6g

Ingredients

2 fresh bananas, sliced
¼ cup wholemeal flour (for dusting)
1 cup wholemeal self-raising flour
1 tablespoon white sugar

1 teaspoon No Egg Egg Replacer
1 cup lactose-free milk
50g butter
Lactose-free cream (for serving)

Remarkable Dental

The team at Remarkable Dentistry in Peterborough, South Australia, pride themselves on providing high quality and comfortable dental care in a modern and relaxed environment.

1. Dust three quarters of the sliced bananas in the ¼ cup of wholemeal flour until they are coated.

2. For the batter, in a bowl combine the 1 cup of wholemeal flour with the egg replacer, milk and sugar. Whisk vigorously.

3. Melt butter in a frypan on medium heat.

4. Dip the banana pieces in the batter and place in the frypan; cook on each side until golden brown.

5. Serve with the lactose-free cream and the remaining banana slices.

Banana Delight

Dr Philip Tan's
Delicious Ice Cream

Delicious homemade ice cream using fresh Australian fruits to share with family and friends.

 10 mins preparation
Overnight to set

 Serves 14 scoops
Serving size: 2 scoops (75g)

 Gluten-free

 Sugar per serve: 4g
Sugar per 100g: 5.3g

Ingredients

400g fresh Australian peaches
400g fresh Australian strawberries
Note: Try the fruit before using to ensure it tastes sweet. Using naturally sweet tasting fruit will guarantee your ice cream has a sweet flavour.
600ml thickened cream
Pinch of salt

1. Place the fruit into a blender and mix to purée.

2. Stir in the thickened cream and place into an ice cream maker or a freezer-safe food storage container.

3. Place the ice cream in the freezer and enjoy once frozen.

Tip: starting with frozen fruit can make the freeze time shorter.

Dr Philip Tan

Dr Philip Tan is a specialist prosthodontist and avid foodie from Bayside Dental Specialists in Cheltenham, Victoria.

Dr Susan Cartwright's
.... Berry Pancakes ....

Fun for kids - a quick family treat.

 15 mins   Makes 12 pancakes
Serving size: 4 pancakes (100g)   Sugar per serve: 3.3g
Sugar per 100g: 3.3g

Ingredients

1 cup self-raising flour
1½ stevia (equivalent to ¼ cup caster sugar)
1 egg
½ cup milk
40g butter
½ cup fresh berries of your choice
Whipped cream and extra berries to serve

Dr Susan Cartwright

Dr Susan Cartwright is qualified as a general dentist and is the Scientific Affairs Manager at Colgate-Palmolive.

1. Melt the butter.

2. Place the flour, stevia, egg, milk and butter in a bowl and whisk until smooth.

3. Add the berries (chopped if large e.g. strawberries) to the pancake batter and stir to combine.

4. In a frypan over a medium heat, melt approximately one tablespoon of butter then cook tablespoons of the mixture for 2-3 minutes on each side until golden.

5. Serve with whipped cream and extra berries.

Natalie Yassa's
········ Homemade Spiced Granola ········

Enjoy this sweet breakfast treat with plain Greek yoghurt and fresh fruits for a healthy, tooth-friendly breakfast.

 15 mins preparation
25 mins baking
15 mins cooling

 Makes 13 serves
Serving size: 40g

 Sugar per serve: 5.8g
Sugar per 100g: 14.4g

Ingredients

2 cups traditional oats
1 cup raw almonds, roughly chopped
½ cup walnuts, roughly chopped
⅓ cup shredded coconut
¼ cup pepitas/pumpkin seeds

2 teaspoons cinnamon
1 teaspoon mixed spice
1 teaspoon fine salt
1 tablespoon orange rind

½ cup coconut oil, melted
100g honey
1 teaspoon vanilla extract

Natalie Yassa

Natalie Yassa is a second year dental student at La Trobe University in Bendigo, Victoria.

1. Pre-heat the oven to 175°C.

2. Line a large tray with baking paper.

3. Add all dry ingredients to a large bowl and mix, ensuring the spices are well incorporated.

4. Mix the wet ingredients in another bowl.

5. Add the wet ingredients to the dry ingredients and mix thoroughly until every dry ingredient is coated.

6. Add the granola mixture to the lined tray and spread it evenly with a spoon. Press down firmly to create more granola clusters.

7. Bake for 25 minutes or until golden, stirring halfway through to ensure the mixture cooks evenly and does not burn.

8. Allow the granola to cool, undisturbed.
   Note: the granola will crisp as it cools.

9. Enjoy with Greek yogurt and fresh berries. Store in an airtight container.

Get Sugar Savvy
Read the label

No added sugar ≠ sugar free

One serve contains 20 grams (5 teaspoons) of sugar

Nutrition Information	
Serves per packing: 1	Serve size: 250ml
Energy	417.5kJ
Protein	1.5g
Fat, total	2g
- Saturated	0g
Carbohydrates	22.25g
- Sugars	20.5g

Beware: Products that claim '**no added sugar**' can still contain **a LOT of sugar**.

Did you know drink fruit juice, the recommended serving size is 125ml of 100% fruit juice? Eating whole fruits and drinking water is a better choice for healthy teeth.

Types of sugar

Natural sugar

- Natural sugar refers to the sugar that is naturally present in whole, unprocessed foods and drinks.

- Examples:

Fruit   Milk   Yoghurt (unflavoured)

It may also be called *intrinsic sugar*.

Added sugar

- Added sugar is sugar added to foods and drinks during processing, cooking or before eating or drinking.

- Examples:

Maple syrup   Coconut sugar   Brown sugar   Rice malt   Sucrose (white sugar)

- Limit added sugar consumption to 6 teaspoons (24 grams) or less, per day.

Natural vs added sugar. Can they affect my teeth the same?

Yes. However, foods such as fruit and milk are made up of small amounts of natural sugars as well as fibre, vitamins and minerals which are good for the body. Milk also includes calcium, which can help to protect the teeth and bones. Processed foods with large quantities of added sugar often have no or limited nutritional value.

Shinal Naicker's
Vegan Banana Bread

Follow Shinal on Instagram at @sugar_diaries, in her Makin. Bakin. Cakin. Adventures!

 20 mins preparation
20-25 mins baking
5 mins cooling

 Makes 8 slices
Serving size: 1 slice (85g)

 Vegan

 Sugar per serve: 9g
Sugar per 100g: 10.6g

Ingredients

3 tablespoons olive oil
100ml soy milk
2 tablespoons apple cider vinegar
4 teaspoons rice malt syrup
2 medium bananas

2 cups plain flour
1 teaspoon cinnamon
½ teaspoon nutmeg
2 teaspoons baking powder
1 teaspoon baking soda

2 tablespoons brown sugar
¼ cup walnuts, chopped
15g extra chopped walnuts chopped for topping

Shinal Naicker

Shinal Naicker was previously an Oral Health Therapist and is now a final (5th) year dental student at Charles Sturt University in Orange, NSW.

1. Pre-heat the oven to 180°C and lightly spray an 18cm square baking dish with oil, or line with baking paper.

2. In one bowl, mix all your wet ingredients (olive oil, soy milk, apple cider vinegar and rice malt syrup) and set aside.

3. In another bowl mix all your dry ingredients (plain flour, cinnamon, nutmeg, baking powder, baking soda and brown sugar).

4. Mash bananas and roughly chop walnuts.

5. Add wet ingredients, mashed bananas, and ¼ cup (35g) of walnuts into your dry ingredients and combine.

6. Place mixture into baking dish, ensure to smooth the mixture flat and then sprinkle with remaining, then add remaining walnuts.

7. Bake for 20-25mins (check whether the banana bread is cooked through by testing with a skewer, ensuring it comes out clean).

8. Place on cooling rack for 5 minutes before cutting up.

Dr Julia Moldavtsev's
Chia-ful Cups

'Chias' to your smile! Keep your smile healthy and bright with this tooth-friendly, low-sugar dessert.

 Overnight

 Serves 2
Serving size: 170g

 Dairy-free

 Sugar per serve: 15.3g
Sugar per 100g: 9g

Ingredients

Base
1 cup unsweetened coconut or almond milk
¼ cup chia seeds

Topping
1 cup cashews
½ cup unsweetened coconut or almond milk
1 tablespoon coconut oil
1½ tablespoons cocoa powder
1 tablespoon honey or rice bran syrup
A few pitted dried dates

Garnish
Fresh raspberries
Mint leaves
Flaked almonds

1. To make the base, mix the chia seeds and cup of unsweetened coconut or almond milk. Divide into 2 serving glasses and place into the fridge overnight.
As the mixture is cooling the chia seeds can clump. To avoid this, give the mixture a stir every once in a while in the first 15 minutes of setting.

2. To make the topping, place the of cashews in a bowl of water and soak overnight.

3. The next day, drain the cashews. Place the cashews into a food processor or blender along with the rest of the topping ingredients. Blend until smooth. Take the 2 serving glasses with the chia mixture and divide the topping between them. Garnish with raspberries, flaked almonds and mint leaves. Serve and enjoy!

Dr Julia Moldavtsev

Dr Julia Moldavtsev works at Bite Dental Studios in the Brisbane CBD and also travels with the Royal Flying Doctor Service. She is passionate about dentistry, equal access to healthcare and dessert!

Get Sugar Savvy

Sugar and its effect on teeth

Sugar + bacteria = acid
Acid + teeth + time = tooth decay

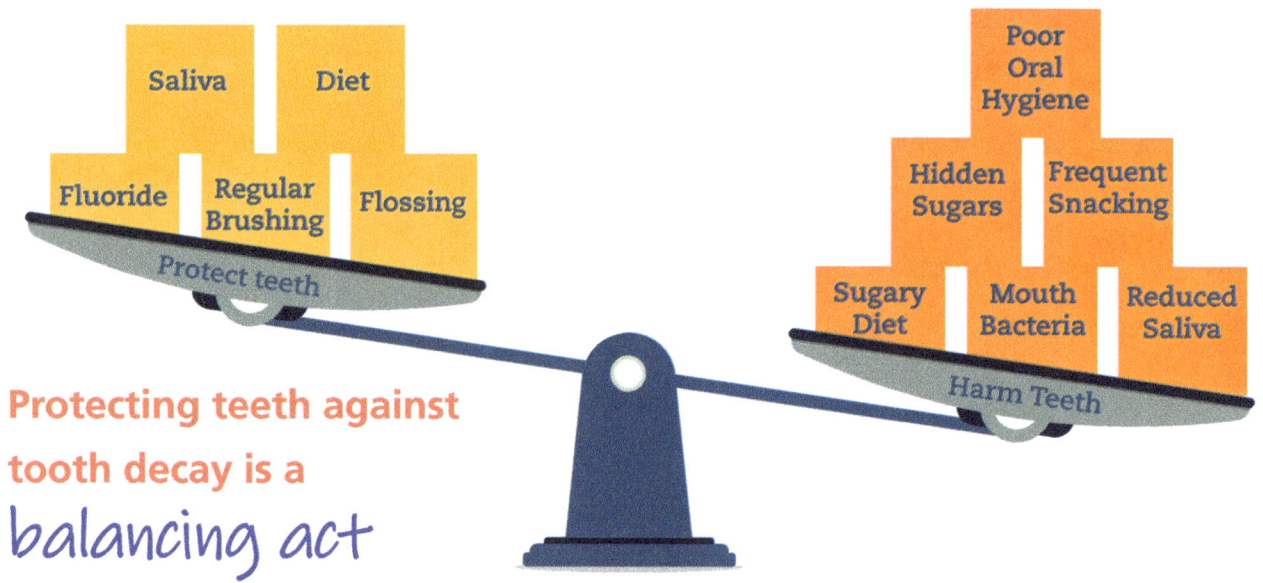

Protecting teeth against tooth decay is a balancing act

When harmful factors outweigh those that protect the teeth, then tooth decay can form.

- Certain mouth bacteria that live on the surface of teeth consume the sugar we eat and turn it into acid.
- The acid sits on the surface of the teeth and pulls minerals out from the tooth's surface causing it to weaken.
- This process happens every time we eat or drink.
- If these acid attacks occur over and over again and there is not enough protection provided to the teeth, this can result in tooth decay.

Go to ada.org.au/tips to watch 'Explaining Tooth Decay', an instructional video explaining how tooth decay forms.

How to protect your teeth:

 Brush twice a day using fluoride toothpaste.

 Consume no more than 6 teaspoons/24 grams of added sugars per day.

 Clean between your teeth once per day.

 Visit your dentist regularly.

Acknowledgement

Thank you to all of the ADA members who entered the recipe competition to create this cookbook for Dental Health Week 2020.

Thank you to Tim from Stiff Chef (@stiffchef) for baking all of the tooth-friendly sweet treats for judging, and to the judges for their hard work in choosing the 20 recipes included within this book.

A special thanks to Annie Jiang for design and Jac Taylor for editing and proofing, helping the ADA's first cookbook come to fruition.